THE COMMONS

THE COMMONS

STEPHEN COLLIS

TALONBOOKS

Talonbooks
P.O. Box 2076, Vancouver, British Columbia, Canada V6B 3S3
www.talonbooks.com

Typeset in New Baskerville and Tribute and printed and bound in Canada.
Printed on 100% post-consumer recycled paper.

First Printing: 2008

The publisher gratefully acknowledges the financial support of the Canada Council for the Arts; the Government of Canada through the Book Publishing Industry Development Program; and the Province of British Columbia through the British Columbia Arts Council and the Book Publishing Tax Credit for our publishing activities.

LIBRARY AND ARCHIVES CANADA CATALOGUING IN PUBLICATION

Collis, Stephen, 1965-
        The commons / Stephen Collis.

Poems.
ISBN 978-0-88922-580-0

        1. Commons–Poetry. I. Title.

PS8555.O4938C64 2008   C811'.54   C2008-901055-8

CONTENTS

"Don't fence me in"
—David Byrne

I.

AT THE FENCE OF POETRY

The Frostworks

Something there is
that spills
makes gaps
the work of
hunters at spring
the wall
between us
is a collapse
of <u>constituency</u>
the boulders
are loaves
we break
together
all is pine
or apple trees
only he says
with nothing
between us
how are we
yet broken

A wall
doesn't love
the frostworks
pressing beneath
or passing
another thing
making disrepair
in gaps widening
having heard
beyond the hill
we walk a line
erasing it as we go

with backs turned
dear fellows
what little need
of this wall
to get across as
neighbours

Something there is
if it is
spring
it is mischief
I could construct
a notion
of others
where before
I built nothing
and to whom
something
wants it down
but he said
in chronology
we appreciate
the part played
by the future
as words not
woods will make
fences or flowing

I wonder friends
isn't it neighbours
in our heads
no cows
only signs pointing
to walling out
I hate a wall
doesn't love
rather see the
alter armed
in shade of trees

that words
are common
as frost or
fences falling
so take a stone
everyone
take a stone
unmending

Is that
frozen ground
a literature
boulders breaking
even two
is another
after them
the yelping dogs
we break
to meet outside
a wall until
fingers come
and I will
orchard
in his pines
till forgiven
all fencing

When across the lines
I like to think
as ice storms do
loaded with rain
as the breeze
soon shattering
such heaps
you'd think
they are dragged
so low you may see
years afterwards
like abandonment
but I was going
with all her matter
as he went
whose only summer
he took to conquer
and not to learn
and not to clean
the ground of branches

Beyond these
frozen forms
frets of others
unknowing
creates cold
film upon waters
a writing of sorts
interrupts the
world was the
strangest thing
winter had in
chorus passed so low
flushed into darkness
started to think
they could not
they must
break into entry
twist daylight
its wind-torn life
again to swoon beneath

Where is joined
the hunter and
the gun
the harvest too close
the fur-things
across the threshold
taking the widespread
advantage revolt has
over reform
they could almost be
forgotten who slept
one night only
in the old barn
its only windows
bullet holes
like waking alone
and checking
its locks against
conservatives

It comes of
wind and winters
dear energy
something there is
isn't just
yours or mine
but between
the light of
eerie dawn or
dusk I coat
the fresh rockery
with movements
and maybe
stone fish fibre
crack block breath
bends leans turns
this onto that
in structure
I'm leaning
into you too

Dear Common

Right of Shack

In Essex attacked tax commissioners
1381 marched on London
out of Essex teaming streams
through Aldgate past Chaucer's apartment
burnt John of Gaunt's palace & Fleet Prison too

To Subdue Finchley Common

Mere to be to be mere lane
fold my course over easement edges
census tax and counsel commons
note the noteworthy but not the unnamed
progress is as progress does
all of us all all of us calling
down the town fringe to fence
O fence us not to fringe our senses
shillings for a single pasture
submitting not the yoke of improvement

To Compel Epping Forest

Can you own the waters pouring?
pour a pail into your pocket
lake I have you by a string
purse is bursting   waters astray
what is proper?   fall in forever
it seeks the lowest place of all
and turns governance into guidance
look it's leisure   taking it slow
dive in fools dive in dive in
your pockets purses fresh as freshets
I am called Nameless Wildness
like strange sparrows winging west
let us have one purse between us

To Conquer Hounslow Heath

Poverty rules them out as lenders
some geese on the common waste to wander
enclosure came as *coup-de-grâce*
poverty nakedly visibly property
labour less the haze of which
liberty lease for couch's potato
so primitive is as accumulation does
right itself out of the sands of time
pleasantly peasants renting fences

Winstanley on George's Hill (1649)

Wind and shadow take away voices
ranting digging and levelling wastes
houses built and rainshowers falling
some have bread so some leave envy
is that voices channeling anger?
carriages lakes and vales of plenty
can I have some? no nonsensical
they are the without having any
deny them not the earth in common
indigenous dust and colonial calumny
the singing of the victor's spoils
owners fencing and indigenous despair

If you wish to carve up sir
the commons & the wastes of poetry
keeping in or keeping out
floor of words whispering treadle
then you've met your pamphleteer
squatting on the lexical common

At the Fence of Poetry

1807 for coming into a garden
and orchard with hatchets
throwing down fences
digging up the ground
and erecting a tent to keep
the pretended owner out

1774 for entering a garden
throwing down fences and hedges
and carrying off garden stuff

1794 at streatham common
six men in black drove up
in a hackney coach and demolished
the duke's paled inclosure

Winstanley Adieu

Thus the work we are going about is this
the nutting & the plough portend
the future lifts its sleeves belief
nothing up my sleeve but grief
from futures I have come to hear
your voices conjure ampliture
beginning's accumulations stint
none that spoke or wrote till hearing
while we spoke from cabins squatting

I commence to bring you hope
I commence to open arms
I commence being at your side
I commence to share your harms
water water please lead me to water
to wash the Earth small stone that was
a common treasury made for all

II.

THE COMMONS

Clear as Clare

"I had imagind that the worlds end was at the edge of the orison & that a days journey was able to find it so I went on with my heart full of hopes pleasures & discoverys expecting when I got to the brink of the world that I could look down like looking into a large pit & see into its secrets the same as I believed I could see heaven by looking into water"

—John Clare

foot-foundered
clover-trussed
homeless at home

wheat-thresher
bird-scarer
lime-burner too

years addicted
to poetical prosing
walking out of magnetism
in an iron file

croft / forct … merely a meaning
swept / swaily … heaven unfenced

owed much to a
golden russet

leeks in the thatch
as a charm against lightning

handing out handbills
to Jacobins in the street

foundry's foundling / flusk for the fields

the fields!
our church
the thirsty pasture
in varied tints
green ripening grain
and blue corn bottles
meadow lake and
marshy fern
sleepers peeping
round orizon's rim

a little patch of common
buckled to my bread
the woodpecker sweeing
flags flaze and flitting

said arable
said commons
said cottage rushlight
clouted dipples stirtling

dim to the seem

at night ... hounding home

fallow
      common
            meadow
closd
      common
            stubble
fallow
      rows

far far far as they ay they field
swallows swallows / firetail and finch

old quarry
swordy well
lip tipped and vetted
pilfering hedgerows
sheep and dale
roly poly scriptor est
botanized and abetted
rough grass
to trim lawn
remains disinhabited

lathy of ramping   ...   jinny-burnt-arse
to hing pleachy sexpools

degected felicitous nonce
biograph of birds
Dr Bottle Imp and Boxer Byron
nice nest, nettles near
older than the earth worms
sounder than the smell
awe apple and flitting
beside old swordy walking west
apple scrumping mixt it twil

Inclosure like a Bonaparte / hung the moles for traitors

bend at being
siding up hedges
places and creeps
the lark starts skylarks
supper! a couple
of flutters on
rawky mornings
covered with rime
(shoot the poets!
pleasantly fences)
harrows painted red
against a dotterel tree

peep a single blossom flower /
that grows in cluster   ...   out of dictionaries the pale

I believe the
French King
cured me
the words
sneering
indefatigable
and if revenge
may the foes
appoint power
ways with success
care for nobody's else

anti-Cromwell
but pro-Robin
I love thee still
while yet a nook is left
unconstrained

his suspicion
the seventeenth century
poetical indignation
the common itself
trees and badgers and birds

pencil work and erasures
gleaning Glinton Marys
a little mad with alliteration
and jogging on from theme to theme
or clare will be no clare no more
clearing furze and fundy moults
a pruning hook took a matter of maisies
asylum poetry / imitation shelley
a gathering of the fugitive
withdrawing non-identity
liberty bitterly and fence offence
poetry an echo home
to press the common air with lungs

nest-left and antsy ... broke on a beam of light

punctuation of open moorland
circling out ripples on a pond

often a line makes equal sense
backwards turning turfs and teasel

punctuation is a ladder
throw it far away falling fell

a sonnet is my elder sister
from the lane to the well ipseity

the latticework commences breathing ease
and we are all turned Frenchmen forward

the advantage of open landscapes falling
portable when placed in apposition to assarts

his head cut off and all the vowels
and consonants taken out one by one

Hail humble
Unlettered waste
where bustling
where dawning
where useless
where fenceless
with frequent forks

Hail scenes
still shall hum
dear native sweet
and oh those dear
those golden
those sports
the vanished green
o'er pebbles
waters and
fallen fences

But now
pleasing pastures
sweet cooling
in dark corners
now all's laid waste
whose cursed weapons
whose victims
whose wants
thou art our labour lost
and woods bow down
to clear a way for thee

Dear beloved spot
what is life?
mad about mergers
dawnings of genius
(ye swampy falls)
the primrose and
the gypsies' evening blaze

we are mostly water swollen /
the other a lake   …   dive in dive in drenching identity

myrtle embanked
my Mary
dithering blea
and besomed
I vanquish fences
forcefully
opening enclosure
Quixote and shivering with cold
dressed up in faux finery
insolvency the only means

eye am a nest   …   in haynish balks
teasle / least and circa cease

there once were springs
like sheets of snow
there once were brooks
the brooks no more

scarce a bush
yon shaggy tufts
as seeming fond
as dreaming sluff

there once were lanes
the spring resembles
enclosure came
to dampen rambles

invert / return / repeat
if you punctuate me comma I will flee

O England
thy poor
like emigrating birds
every village owns
while mongrel clowns
disdain thy lawns
ye fields
ye meadow-blooms
ye banished trees
the paléd road
naked scenes drew
spreading thorns
and bramble bounds
I've crosst out of me
five measures and a mile
the leek in the thatch
lightens mine mind

little field
    I   swagger
my little plough
    I leave a sign
behind the
   mouldywarps
     the field   remains
murmuring complaints

little parcels / little minds
with cowslips smothered … out behind

enclosure
comfort's cottage soon

workplace prisons
her sacred dower

the common heath
the spoilers prey

music making elm
rights of freedom

they overwhelm
who glut their vile insatiate maws

shh I'm fleasting … out mongst many melt
lake / kale and ampl / lamp … mild limd we wander

To the snipe:

furze cloud
russet clods
wing neath
searing turf

peep nash
dustmill whisp
pismire sock
and scatter shank

fermety stulp
o'er shipwreck strange

I mutter between ... two asylums

returned home out of essence
and found no Mary

down the lane gently
where being night

a green paddock
began to stagger

being rather weak
got to a village and forgot the name

returned home out of essence
having disowned none

seeing a stone
was very painful

the good natured
suddenly recollecting elm trees

the wind came
and the road began to light

hobbled shutters a sort of shed
the people up and dark

returned home out of essence
and found it led to London

standing under the hedge
I could see no tree or bush

hummed the air
alone near a wood

the sign seemed to stand oddly
nest nest all gone to roost

returned home out of essence
till daylight and fell

down on a flint heap
to keep up the crown

so weary awhile
to rattle up recollection

myself eating the grass
tasting something of bread

foot-foundered and broken down
making for the beehive as fast as I could

Blackberries

thrust out backward bramble common
no visible fairyland utopian terse
my companion and I along
blue wall sudden as children
throwing the baby in red
dress frozen the quilted thrush
no other interest save pecuniary
voluntary huckle berry party affect
the hedgerow the light dissolving
onto mercury flash paper prints

the owl the sod the
soft gravelly banks elastic nature
confounds vagrant meandering river wrecks
strew bottoms rivulet shrubs nuthatch
thither all birds in woods
spring nights and chickadee lisps
especially for aldermen and epicures
do not feed the imagination
as study out of doors
let alone your garden cease

I am astonished quenching click
focus on bramble berry dell
over against self window us
a vision compelling in part
scattering a legion about one
my companion whispers between berries
the glory of architecture grows
many an unnoticed wild berry
vespertinal habits the walking of
which the springs of life

growing imaginary alternatives to chainlink
marginalia of suburban texts rubus
remains august edges improvements converts
leaves gentrified junk swagged with
fruit taking to the fences
points unjoined canes lines spreading
indefinitely spreading lines curving fruit
centres circumference euclid arcs radius
all right angles are incongruent
infinitely many intersecting commons coil

.to find wind sudden together
along roadside untended curving canes
walk fields wood since selves
those which you have fetched
yourself carry us thither baskets
shake off village return senses
prospect harmony radius never quite
familiar of all large trees
people would begin mere objects
to the state burning fences

a rare red low being
where it grows prickles sparingly
this sound information in fives
sides of canes and leaves
fifth berry of the year
trundled amongst trees to offer
form to swallows songs or
robins trying to recognize the
shape of a nest amongst
tangle of twigs and bramble

found in emerson antennae and
stamina fuller dial rejected downcast
delight and interjected this else
solitary and clear perception was
no apples theft from others
orchard each fruit wild and
independent of any other though
many taken together make a
better tart or with cream
as his almost constant companion

to monopolize the little gothic
window then did I use
with eyes upturned the clouds
to wander in rich drapery
that I might peep a
truant hawk or write a
brief obituary as to what
of the beautiful it had
lived election amongst the plants
feeding all kinds of pensioners

everything miracle spore sated geometry
found equinox thrusting words having
no connection into all parts
of every sentence boot jack
for instance taking liberty nothing
and no place ventured gained
to whit the berries' abundance
how could any contain scarcity
this many hands picking sense
to gather scrutiny shared provenance

in moist woods and thickets
shoots tinge the earth crimson
my liberty is in wandering
to what nothing owns but
blackberries tangle throughout the fringe
up to the town in
trinkets beyond nature's own growth
the fruit which I celebrate
growing everywhere we cannot purchase
leaning into the dark cluster

scituate wandering lines in cool
atmosphere frothed linen sweet attire
the pleasure of gathering together
the wreaths of black fruit
cottonwood smell ripe hawks' truancy
to call crows clatter we
see so much only as
we already possess jointly together
a pronoun a basket bushel
collected selves between no others

thursday they awoke their tents
in a corn barn abandoned
friday dawned clear sunday and
monday devoted to mountains awoke
to find autumn continuing rapidly
downstream wind through haze of
memory purchased an apple pie
nature under a veil there
in town or beaten common
the neglected bramble tangles property

I hear of service berries
poke weed juniper vines dross
the creaking of the earth's
axle where the beauty is
in mosses along dry leaves
or lifting the leaves the
meadow mouse has slept in
the mutter of aperture saying
we only to themselves alone
another memory of strained light

stood clasped in brother's scarlatina
consolation a visiting daguerreotypist dawn
burnt chemical pyre watchful of
nurses and friends goodbyes nimble
the nuthatch unlocked his health
on fences forgotten between properties
the very roadsides a fruit
garden all culture aims to
secure though I've heard of
pickers ordered out of fields

october tinged poetry confounding change
leaves with withered ones ensued
island no concord runs a-blur
look ma no hands triumph
so do leaves the pellicle
earth show of many fruits
which we ignore softening already
in shade till near end
of august thick enough to
pick as some idler's folly

I understand nothing of illness
what grows out against our
other springings this spent thistle
sending its spores adoring leaving
as only a short excursion
look this is a print
of the night sky unfolding
look these are my loved
ones uttering chaos I only
see the beginning of bereavement

earliest reddening woodbine the lake
of radical leaves hickory beautifully
flecked turn over its leaves
and through oaks and aspens
spotted leaves gloaming brakes of
purple grasses red maple elm
fallen sugar scarlet patches glow
I begin to see children
the first ripe blackberries thereabouts
scarcely rising above the ground

lookout shadowy boxers lineage palimpsest
vogue mixt with twillberry oft
picked haversack full of berries
gone to saunter and free
to culture flint the forest
filled on long peduncles lifted
in the shade of pines
different variety from the common
counting berries five a fist
plenty sprung on unwanted easements

built subtle shack on common
turned back clock solitary nary
chipmunk dug borrowed mowed berried
thrift silent merchant spent days
mellowing this captioned self gave
banks mud warmed winged life
those large and late low
whortle spur snare buck prune
run over common dense clusters
clammy acid taste countless variety

true flavor never purchased obtained
lost with the bloom become
mere provender thus finished errand
miles off midst endless berries
nowhere states seen history prisons
amidst sweet fern and sumac
or growing more rankly in
low ground by rich roadsides
what no one owns shared
thus our blackberries remnant commons

The Lakes

"They deem the district a sort of national property,
in which every man has a right and interest who
has an eye to perceive and a heart to enjoy"

—William Wordsworth

"And hereupon, The Earth (which was made to be
a Common Treasury of relief for all ...) was
hedged in to In-closures by the teachers and rulers,
and the others were made Servants and slaves: And
that Earth that is within this Creation made a Com-
mon Store-house for all, is bought and sold, and
kept in the hands of a few"

—Gerrard Winstanley

Directions for the Futurist

Speaker of commons I
take liberty in others
my book would itself free
some little affinity country
in which no property lies

So we make it other measures
often traveled procuring reception
a few improvements difference places
also to others how variously nature
occasioned its little sportive anachronisms

In my address I consider a vehicle
waters portage and the length of logs
my book my vanity and my friend
I hope you excuse my not communicating

Vision's Excursion

The VALES and their lakes too many to
name the general surface pasturage torrents
burstings of water entrench and scar like
letters bluish or hoary grey encrusted the
soil hence down the mountains a dove's
neck tinge the principle of decomposition
tint of the herbage in october travelling
twice the rich usually passes away towards
the summit hues in common colours are
perpetually around them each created
mountain a point to furnish oak coppices
birch stands and hollies center the view

As to the best views
More distant
Fine bird's-eye views
The most stunning views
Conveniently seen from the peer
With a lofty though but slender
Suddenly a fine view
Between projections
The transverse views
Retired views sweet views delicious views
The views, especially
Looking at water
Heights and eminences
Cold pork in their pockets
Views quickly terminated
Again into view
Vales and mountains enclosing
Only mentioned that the transient visitant may know
A view not interrupted
Peculiarly of the eye and sole
The almost visionary mountain republic
Viewed from above
Under Locke and Keynes

Walked with books gathered mosses
Plants supposed it was ranunculus
Flights so round the lake and quietness
Producing ourselves and not forgetting
The stone chats went down rambling
Got Lockety goldings took up plants
Sate upon a stone reading ballads
Hearing sibling's tread thrid the trees
Distant objects faded abjection
Through a gate the lake all blue
And purple and grey in the wood to alter
Poems then read on water to another
Letting the boat take its own course
Arrived home with some slips of privet
Gathered and a page of water stained

We shall now speak of the LAKES the
form of the lake which belongs peculiarly
to the lake the clouds the light all the
imagery of the sky and hill characteristic
of the lakes peculiar form of water present
to the reception of lakes wishing for an
interposition of green meadows trees that
lakes should be little mutual out of sight
upon a lake in winter the lake rises a line
of leaves and leavings surface passes fence
posts and surrounds smooth deposits of
otherwise men may not threaten adorned
dwindle their flat desolate habituations of
however the lakes turn meandering shores
fertile vales   let us rather in imagination
the cultivation of flat or mountain among
bays of fine blue or upon reeds and bul
rushes exposed to gleaming with no certain
rim

No one voice to fence a limit
To be guided and not to guide
To pose and not to repose
The insurgent waters force is fleeting
To be many leagues in circumference
A mirror not mirrored in cold reflection
The lakes pool on archive shelves
Labouring mimetic denial to trees
And description's deformation
Lead us leftward out of purchase

Other lakes part of this lake extremity of
the lake surface of the lake the lake is
generally visit the lake only lake and
crossed the lake broken view of the lake
in some situations limpid lake lake from
the lake may side of the lake margin
embraces lake stretching river and lake
broken by hedgerows copses order the
lake upon the lake only down the lake
cross the lake genius of the lake banks
of the lake the lake situated obtained a
prospect of the lake the lake lies over
looks the lake purchased vantage from
the lake bosom of the lake sweeps the
lake denying may to august watering
haven tints from trees and aerial hues
the lake looking many glens its lake and
open impending woods the lake you
both lake and rocks on the lake murmurs
falling this lake vocal echoes lakes such
lakes altogether and capture the sight

This lake claude glass
Capturing mountains picturessence
Bough bend and the economy of
Logs and displaced indigeny

Repose on property
Contemplation's waters
Bought and sold
Walkers now a form of dispersal
Accumulating primitives guard the view
Water one day as valuable as oil is now

Wordsworth and West lie in the foreground
The lake in the middle distance lies
Then the ancient oil wells creaking
At the built and bordered orizon

How many roots amongst the writer flight
of swans geese or ducks the pen sees
wantonly brings springs full of green
shimmer to the page lets the water lead
or the hand the finger drag the surface
as boat glides through the commons where
fence meets shore only a reflecting line
ripples out onto the water the logs on the
bottom are owned the dock jutting out
of privacy makes a shadow but the liquid
meadow between is what we drink and
swim in naked blue and all queerly alike

Abandoning the Long S

Elegant snake like curve of black
Water in narrow dark arm
Adopted in certain scriptoria
To dive or swim across at night
Crossbar extending only to the left
West arm where docks and boats propelled
Foulis varia prolusions in Madrid
Paddled there past dark to part
By changes that were stealing over
Mink or otter or mere raccoon scat
Hath ventured to depart the common mode
J stroke in which the thumb turns towards the keel
Where the bee sucks the lines seem more open
Draw to pull the water towards the hull
Changes stealing printing lakes and lines
Pry the water away from the side
Willingness to sweep the s from their cases
Sweep a wide stroke out in an arc
Threw off speculators in typography

At camp every beginner or found a boat to steal
Newly literate working classes saw a confusing
And old fashioned character
Grabbed gunnels when tipped too far
Victim of the 1799 Seditious Societies Act
Drove late at tremble down the arm
Still reserved for cheap and ephemeral publications
Drove late away in forbidden boats
And thereby tranfmit to pofterity
The last light lingering to the weft
Most printers embracing the modern look
To the weft seen best by boat
As the paring of all men's noses
The mountain eaft but the last light weft
Revivals for its picturesque associations
The weft totally filent ftill
Left therefore deftroying time
With the variations that have happened
The diffolution of the rights
Privileges and cuftoms of the tenants

which i

west. These,

gloom were

The ſun was
Viſible
But had fired the whole
Weſtern orizon
A deep red
With grey tints
& ſtrong ſhadows
& the weſt a
theſe glowing in the deep

tract, which is
the manner he defigned
language &
thefe books
thefe grounds
thefe natural beauties
& the mouths
& their accidental beauties

thefe fcenes penetrated

decorated with iflands

where Mr. Gray ftood
enchanted regions the
contemplative traveller afcends

thefe parts
thefe particulars
thefe lie to the weft

—inclofures—c

ind, above al

The Social Lake

Dear hereditary sub-tenants
drove out en masse
a few roods and cottages clinging
sides of lakes and
permissive pasture
I spindle thwarts of
nonsense profits
cast off trace of common lands
vindicated rights and private estates
annexed to new bankocracy
whilst the place was ever taken
for sole pleasure of the landlords
thus I give a few extracts
and enclose my common name

I divorce you sad producer
says the primitive accumulations
of my capitalist harp
strung with strings of blood and fire
property was paucity
(hey, I forgot to own!)
when enjoying the usufruct
of the common land
prelude of the revolution was
usurpation of said commons
into sheep-walks boundary stones

Creation's tenant farmer
luxuriant plain water
common ferrugineous clay
freestone turf wall
the several vestiges
of ancient boundaries
commoning together protects

Attachment to letters
called our attention
on eden we paddled
deep repose by
blue expanse of distant objects

This liquid sheet
writ crystal road
admitting frequent peeps
and many points of
interest gathered in
luxuriant banks
steep declivity and a
verdant rising sprinkled
with a few cottages

this slight sketch of two branches
accelerated by capital
you mean you like old dictions too?
invigorating teasel tense
yours & etc.

The storm of affection over
I alighted surrounding abundance

For cottage interest
the other I regret
except the island is my home
visited by material convulsion
so in hopes of a more genial season
peasants dissolving fences rising
with umbrellas in their hands

Before Canoes to Memory

Before canoes to memory
the water was every I
lived there to linger the
tops of firs to wag
the water's own surface
drinks a paddle splash
was summer or a fall
for raking the grass to
now and water to plunge
my quenchless visions to
people time or a trout
to jump or crystal
reflection along the logs
own bobbing shadow look
bobolink I don't know
your name but we share
this love of fresh water
and forest fringe the
air with fire's brief flight

Before canoes to memory
but privilege permits access
property contained border
another bodied water
tribe of brothers sister
I am swimming the
liquid archive chutes
luddite paddles streammouth
and I wonder what has
become of our comrades
whose shape was also water

Before canoes to memory
where my language leaks
boats trains beginners
and life vests valise
trundled letters knee-high ferns
sky storms surface
winds to lift oars to stroke
mundane magic quiet walks
the water near witches weathers
I drift a boat to begin being
drift a boat to recall reeds
a little boat is small pleasure
but I'd give it you the same
to drift elements without envy
give it you a little boat
and the wind we'd share the lake
or take turns at solitary leisure

Paselt

Come metropolitan poets
teach us what is fixed
fleeting transitory being
this labour   art   understanding
image of genuine freedom
the tree tipping over our
home at grass merely depreciates
whatever properties we have
nothing to measure against
paradise of common spousal
would proclaim nothing individual
or with blended might
near others' fields and groves
topple into tenancy

In what vale
shall we turn open field
the very words singled out
imperfect sound
Sweet Vale in common
by Milton left
to dwindle liberty
Dear ghosts through fields
a deep radiance of signs
values vale its hollows hung
so others' toils became prey
amongst the solitary hills

Discordant society
tether lake to mountains
in cadence little boat
mooring meadows
set visible cottage
for all imitative pleasures
lowly cottage ministrations
with pencil parcelled
in verse gleaming monarchs
the impassioned lake
the bond of union
threw huts to fancies
linking kindred water
like a forgotten common
the chance collisions
unions work

So said henceforth
let each keep not to his station own
nor in pity false but form
in inofficious brotherhoods
where none needs
and all are active
and Stolen and Perverted Writings
are the new age
and once more erect
the standard of advantage all

Poet was I on earth th
but was I renowned
was I
as yet my vocal spirit
drew to herself
I deserved myrtle
the peoples name
Chiapas and Grasmere
the seeds ardour the sparks s
which heated me
of need speak I
to nurse in song
this weighted I
and to have lived
more than I must

What candles or what sun
rebels towards   Parnassus
who bears his light behind
makes wise the persons after
through the I poet was
word after word after
removed periods of thoughts passage
unto human hunger revolving
I perceived their hands
their wings as well

Without speech and hearing
for a long time I went
failing to find or foreclose
enclosed lands I am property
the fire fed with looking
amongst folk to purify me not
thou leavest footprints in me
words efface them
what cause in wood and look
those dulcet lays
long endure fashion
their very ink O
sister
I point out
the tongue a better smith
of love and proses

Words' Worth

Become a resident of that Poetic Region
I labor suin   I labor leate weary lover
natural artist   this land is your land but
I've bought it now   let the tourist lack an
access   leeching living here is swearing
leaving none gather linger   soon about
waters we fall into reflection   that me
was we in my private version   vision
impedes not the soul   colonized description
and guided to death   leaping now we're
all fishes   forest hound and matters blank

Now all voices are his own   the poem not a
nation's property   but a commons all can
share   bring me a cup of this every day
bring me a bay and a boat for democracy
bring me swimmers bring me waters   the
subtle and the stolen weft   nothing but
their numbers swollen   and their shouts
and cannonballs crashing

Breeze lake motion
so very lake
stir lake a sage
lake a flock of sheep
when lake a roe
more lake a man
lake clouds sound
lake thunder was
lake of light
lake the solemn shelter
by noble privilege lake
soul lake music
lake a book in memory
lake rivulets in may
lake a garment wear
lake a whirlwind
each being common
sister of our hearts
crest lake Dian's when

Dear Vale my home
lights by a fire jutting lake bottom
mossed rock swimming hole
Sister our voices ripple
rocks concentric rings
to light feeble leaf
leans over summer
red winged blackbird
I know you sister dream
tornadoes and this cottage closure
nights ahead to darken dawn
out amongst the shore frogs shout
croaking I have dreamt a boat
a little boat I sail at night
past the cottage hills and vale

Built a cabin in an archive
squatting amongst the shelves array
the lakes in manuscript
scattered before me
mist a word I barely see
the verdant mountains were a frame
(the eye enclosed its assessed value)
and authors thefe the words their names
authors thefe books and bargains
weft a sheet to write on water

Go my lakes we've sold you property
go to flooding the planters and dredgers
swimmers are your poets now
the picturesque is an enclosure
as the author is as well
words' value is in words' freedom
words are what we share between
swimming language lake we squat on
meanwhile my hope to fetch from failure
collective ghosts of collectivity
and undo the lockes from persons properties

I had a lake or
fhould I fay a
lake had me to
barter its bay

And fome words
fell forth and
gave a boat to
fteal to crofs to

fteal a thwart

And all was writ
on water names
improper fo no
property came

now juft this letter
links lake to ink
our craft is gone
our words do fink

marsh daisy havver grass
woats dog burk tree
horse nops bur thistle
unlik fence codlins cream
esh lily goose grass
rennet button twitch turf
in the north I am said
liquorice Spanish whist ibed
chary rattan trail tops
bottle of all sorts and
sour dockins wineberries mess
choops chubem hine bilt
arse-smart bity tongue
hen drunks and meg wi' many
common mallow wallow mourn

Thus hill-walking held nervous Romantics
or that hintering was barely known
before a leisured bourgeois began
to notice the close of the eighteenth century
Ta-dah!

Uncanny rockfall cheered eccentric applause
we vote on intimations and brook landslides
the colours of lichen moss crystal and vapour

as ey in meyne and theyne
craa and haak and the long o
crothet and sothet
aapral es cruddle moot
moam tips jenny brunt
cowper hand and cowper word
nip to nwote and inkle duck
I'm gone back gone by sel
fliar flinders fo by noon
I'm apt to druck a doggert wark
or skrike the punder hote

The springing crops and domestic beasts
their place by his poem's permission
authors fields with fences failings
and copyrights his name the lake adorns

Once granted the mountains pressed into service
aesthetic barricades leap to city quietude
while the saint in the foreground seems
but the excuse for the mountains in the background
thus I enamel these plates for your taste
merely hoping you'll be angered to action

History is almost wholly silent
wolf-grey head hid in the clouds
and is the common carriage road
yet they lose their summits sky
ill effects of burgage tenure
the place the judges of assize
opened by a rude balustrade

White-hart tree is probably liberal
they remain as monuments elapsed
I like to think I lived here lonely
the lake itself saluted the eye
born a red-winged blackbird warble
distance of the gaze to measure naught
to the left the lake spread out
all its properties breeze and glitter
to the left the vale winds from sight
they had occasion to lament
the lake the weft the owner's papers

III.

from *THE BARRICADES PROJECT*

Dear Common: Letter from Being

"dear beings, I can feel your hands"
—Robin Blaser

It speaks the among
to itselves
as forged creation is
complex things
something insofar as
the nothing appearing
or the among
small significances are
posited where location comes
to *traverse* originality
so we will us in a world
but it speaks back
the being of if

"Strangeness" is access
to the "thing"
to us that access
is a folded mass
is this "the arts"
among themselves
sealed transportable
and solute as a sign?

Originary things
"doves" and "stones"
other bodies
exteriority *in me*
movements posing the
world is variations
you blink at beginning
where it is furnished
means and ends
we wither against
supporting being
as a between us hence

Allow me turning
person a place
and vanishing
a pebble magic
if we do but seek
destructive rage
in the other
our exclusion
terested in
the desire for origin
for all cruelly
a pale wonder
"spark spark"
I am bits
little swarms of
matter

The theme of
exception is
velvet paradox
just where meaning is
their coexistence
little charity, a wind
opens waterways
within being
the arts strange existence
as etymology's
Basque or Arabic elegance

As we so we
so we become
all fruit of ventures
usufruct
America America
Locke was wrong
persons not properties
but singular plural
we are as
sheep or deer
bounding
so we are we
so we become

I enter density
on the page
the maculate weight
of eternity's strain
here is my politics
stone-blind it
lifts getherness to my ear
listening to difference's
strange measures
strange attractors
I am one with you
many and abroad

Dear Common: *¡Ya Basta!*

This is our simple word
this is why we said enough
thievery governments and the world
joined forces silence
beamed straight forests
groves together willing boughs
trained in politics and in weapons
until we set aside the fire
and took up words' other lightnings

Through such as resisted well
deceit of decaf and bad governments
mountain guerillas and drenching languages
I'll download your rebellion
but my virus makes actions properties
buying up the domains of freedom
and surveiling the lines of defence

Everything law locked in constitution
I like these leaves left unknown
discarded agreements and attacked Acteal
bad governments vs intergalactic *encuentros*
invited others planets didn't come
perhaps they did they did
not make it clear
the mountains resistance and
indigenous commons
siege of the village by its own inhabitants
absentee expropriation
primitive as 1649 / 1994

Hearts of others uncontained
it was as if seeing in mirrors
ourselves others uncontained
lazy politician parasite
look the ground is dragged by snakes
overcome we weep as rivers
nothing never leaves the land
washing topsoils clearcuts oceans
we hold on self-governing communities
to the sides of mountains' ruins
would be better with nothing below
just everything level levelling
Zapatistas soldiers so there
won't be any soldiers more
and govern obeying has continued
for we fought to be free
not change masters electioneering

Let us propose post-capitalism
I am leaning towards new intents
this *selva* freed ends meeting
we are heavy with doubt and direction
land evictions to smashing unions
enclosure's wet genetic dreams
genetic coding and thoughts of freedom
I own that smirk so pay up buddy
deregulation so they may profit
we are woods on fire with words
standing here the seduction is electric
pay my bills and call my lawyer
if we are ever even we are free
not to mention no one owns saying
we withdraw our labour and consent
from commanding heights of the economy

I choose solidarity and find no purchase
out on plains equal to horizons
we pass sandbags from one continent
to another rallying deluge
invest in nothing but siblings welfare
all have proven aspects of capitalism
trying new forms of shaping assemblies
try *encuentros* electric *ejidos*
baker's dozen and surplus value
pocket rents in civic fabric
we pass paving stones one street
to another city by city fitfully flawed
peasant pre-proletarian to say
nothing of needles and addicted parks
pretending to work for pretend pay
sometimes I don't feel I have access
utopia was never an invitation to velvet
I attach to a class and rig dejection
thus odes are not necessary to solidarity's delight
we're choosing we as the choice of belonging
now there are many to calculate crops
openly attempting to entirely opt out

If there is to be
civil society every abound
if uncivil we
tamper with capital's course
and communications sound
and if borders redesigned
designer genes
if freight's deregulation informs
if cheap clothes and coffee is cool
then we take to the barricades voice
if elections then electric communiqués
if enclosed feasts
then hacking fences firewalls
if tariffs tools then
appropriating and disseminating
calls against singleness and
idle leisure remote pleasures properties
and if we are sold only singleness then
channel others' unending rage

Another possible world
melts forest's metals
January 1994 myriad strokes
2005 *sexta declaración*
against this neoliberal lesion
well and truly screwed *campesinos*
we think that perhaps our we
sin tierra modus operandi
just remain quiet shushing leaves
our email addresses ascend
to a light on the left look
and a light was called Che
so send some non-transgenic maize
or maybe bomb-choked words of resistance
smooth fortress capital hosts
globalize this mendicant dollar
very otherly leaf-bound brother
we are hope's eternal website
very otherly moving coasts
intercontinental and damn proud of it
very otherly at least and yes
very otherly awaiting the dawn

AN INTRODUCTION TO
THE BARRICADES PROJECT

by
Ramon Fernandez and Alfred Noyes

"And just when they seem engaged in revolutionizing themselves and things, in creating something that has never yet existed, precisely in such periods of revolutionary crisis they anxiously conjure up the spirits of the past to their service and borrow from them names, battle-cries and costumes in order to present the new sense of world history in this time-honoured disguise and this borrowed language"
—Karl Marx, *Eighteenth Brumaire of Louis Bonaparte*

"The historian's task is to grasp the constellation which his own era has formed with a definite earlier one"
—Walter Benjamin, "Theses on the Philosophy of History"

We place the above quotations as sort-of-epigraphs to "The Barricades Project"—if such a project could be conceived as having "epigraphs." For to have epigraphs the "Project" would have to have a beginning and, at the very least, a discernable shape to the front of which such epigraphs could be attached. This is the difficulty with "The Barricades Project": it is a borderless structure. It begins and ends nowhere. It is in fact *of* "nowhere" in a very completely incomplete sense. Each act of writing we might choose to include in "The Barricades Project" is a "throwing up of a barricade in language to (temporarily) obstruct a passage in Capital"—or, alternatively, "a casting down of a fence put in place by the language of capital." At least, this is how we understand it, in an ideal sense. Thus, despite being so thoroughly of "nowhere," the "Project's" barricades are thrown up in particular streets, at particular moments, and they are made from particular local materials found at hand. These particularities can be traced, and so one can be permitted to speak of "The Barricades Project," without having a sense of its limits, origins, or ultimate ends.

The words of Marx above indicate the characteristic gesture of the "Project": at a moment of change, a reaching back in order to move forward. "The Barricades Project" insists on this fact shared by poetry and revolutions: dead ends force us to circle back to other streets—streets not yet blocked, streets that might be in need of blockading—streets of possibility, streets of trespass and occupation. It asks of failure, *what was right?* It asks for recovery, reclamation, reconsideration. It makes music from the languages of revolutions past. It choruses out of context. It stops the passage of the One to Itself, revealing the avenues of the mobile Many. It suspects that there is still something unresolved in the words that have been thrown as bricks through the windows of the bourgeois world. Thus, the "past" of interest here is the past of change, a history of willed futures, a history of movements for change.

It would, considering what we have already said, be incorrect to say that "The Barricades Project" "began" with Stephen Collis's *Anarchive*. But it is true that we first discerned its unimaginable outlines there, in that book's address to the "commons" and in its apparent upholding of the situationist adage that "poetry is the revolutionary act *par excellence.*" The shiftiness of the "Project" is perhaps suggested by our inclusion within the pages of *Anarchive* (Ramon for his verse, Alfred for his translations of that verse)—and by the fact that our own work continues, outside the parameters of that book. The "Project" also includes the present volume, but again we demur to call *The Commons* "Book II" of "The Barricades Project." *The Commons* itself is incomplete (for instance, work properly "belonging" to it, such as the poems "Ode on Autonomy" and "A Description of the Lake at Shawnigan," goes uncollected here), and its connection to the "Project" may not be immediately discernable: in *Anarchive* we are clearly in the streets of Barcelona, circa 1936, in the midst of a recognizable revolution; in *The Commons* we are wandering the English countryside with the so-called mad peasant poet John Clare, just escaped from an Essex asylum and walking the more than eighty miles to his home in Helpston, picking wild fruit with primitivist Henry David Thoreau, also newly escaped from jail—for not paying his poll tax—and undermining the English Lake District, and William Wordsworth's proprietary claim upon it, with a host of authors of Romantic *Guides* and *Tours*.

Where, one might ask, are the "barricades" here? They are in the inverse: in the resistance to enclosure (the process by which most of the English common lands were taken, by force and parliamentary decree, out of the hands of local, collective use), in the tearing down of property's fencing, in a wandering search for new commons, new spaces outside of property's exclusive and excluding domain. The resistance to capital's "primitive accumulation," registered in peasant revolts of the fourteenth through eighteenth centuries, failing to hold off the tide of what we now call "privatization," spilt over into literary romanticism's own advocacy of a kind of commons. Underground in "the literary" since the nineteenth century, the fight against enclosure resurfaces today amidst continuing accumulations, new enclosures, and a renascent sense of the commons under globalization.

A further note on the commons. A commons is not so much an alternative to the system of private property as it is the *absence* of the private. It is not collective *ownership* but collective use of the unowned, unownable, of that which exists outside the dynamics of property and capital. Common lands are held in trust by everyone and governed only by local custom. They embody sustainability and the sharing—commoning—of the resources such sustainable communities depend upon. To enclose the commons was to bring it within the precincts of property—to make it property—exclusive, singular, fenced—a source of private wealth rather than collective well-being. This happened with land centuries ago. It is happening now with water and air, with ideas and genetic coding and materials—with the ineffable essences of life. In so far as a literature takes on a practice of quotation, collage, allusion and intertextuality it holds out a sort of commons— a page on which any may write with the common resources of the poetic past.

We can speak only haltingly of the future of "The Barricades Project." There is to be a *Red Album* situated somewhere in and around Paris, 1789 to 1968 (with stops between). There will no doubt be other works about whose connection to the "Project" we can only speculate (Margaret Fuller on the ground in Rome, 1848?). We do not even know if we ourselves are its agents or outcasts, avatars or exiles. We leave this to others. "Liberty is calling you back to your language." "Here we are, the dead of all times."

In regard to the present volume, consider, if you will, the following scene. Two figures stand on a precipice over this book. One wears a simple, rough peasant's smock. The other, military fatigues. One carries a farmer's hoe, the other an automatic rifle slung under his arm. One has a hand-made straw hat upon his head, the other a black knit balaclava pulled down over his face. The ground they stand upon is variously called St. George's Hill or the Lacandon Jungle. It is 1649 and 1994. All time's peasantry pin a hope. Move onto the former common and begin to dig. Move onto the road and throw up a barricade. Dear Common, the we we are telling has told us all the same. Yesterday, today, tomorrow. Some place in a poem.

—Barcelona & Vancouver, Spring 2007

ACKNOWLEDGEMENTS

This book is for all those working on poetry's common.

Thanks to: Andrea Actis, Mike Barnholden, Colin Browne, Peter Burrough, Pauline Butling, Weyman Chan, Jeff Derksen and Sabine Bitter (Not Sheep), Simone Dos Anjos and Pietro Aman, Roger Farr, Susan Howe, The Kootenay School of Writing, Joshua Kotin, Glen Lowry, Rob Mclennan, Donato Mancini, Jay Millar, Sachi Murakami, Shiri Pasternak (The Commons Conference), Nicholas Perrin, Lisa Robertson, Jordan Scott, Fred Wah, Lissa Wolsak, and Jerry Zaslove. Thanks to Betty Schellenberg, Margaret Linley, and Michelle Levy for their work on the Lake District. Thanks to Tony Power and Eric Swanick in SFU's Special Collections.

Thanks also to the editors of the journals in which work from *The Commons* has appeared: *Chicago Review*, *The Modern Review*, *Parser*, and *West Coast Line*. Thanks to Bookthug for publishing *Blackberries* as a chapbook in 2005.

And thanks, finally, to my parents (and grandparents) for fifty years of Shawnigan Lake, and to Cathy, for enduring my obsessions.

*

The Commons is a field formed on the edge of many other texts. I name just a few of them here.

"Clear as Clare": *I Am: The Selected Poems of John Clare*, ed. Jonathon Bate; *John Clare: A Biography*, by Jonathon Bate; *Edge of the Orizon: In the traces of John Clare's 'Journey out of Essex,'* by Iain Sinclair.

"Blackberries": *Walden and Resistance to Civil Government*, and *Wild Fruits*, by Henry David Thoreau; *The Days of Henry Thoreau*, by Walter Harding.

"The Lakes": *The Prelude*, "Home at Grasmere," and *A Guide to the Lakes* by William Wordsworth; *A Guide to the Lakes*, by Thomas West; *The Grasmere Journals* of Dorothy Wordsworth; *A Tour Through the Northern Counties of England*, by Richard Warner; *Tours of the British Mountains*, by Thomas Wilkinson; *Observations on Several Parts of England*, by William Gilpin; The British Tourists, by William Mavor; *A Journey Made in 1794*, by Ann Radcliffe. John Milton via Ronald Johnson. Statius via Dante.